AMAZING GRACE!

PAUL'S GOSPEL MESSAGE TO THE GALATIANS

BRIAN JOHNSTON

Published by:

HAYES PRESS Publisher, Resources & Media,

The Barn, Flaxlands

Royal Wootton Bassett

Swindon, SN4 8DY

United Kingdom

www.hayespress.org

Table of Contents

CHAPTER ONE: THE PURE GOSPEL (GALATIANS 1:1-11)

Andrew Parker lay across a damaged walkway and formed a human bridge allowing 20 people to walk to safety over his body above the ice-cold waters of the North Sea. This happened half an hour after the Herald of Free Enterprise ferry had left its berth in the Belgian port of Zeebrugge. The ferry had set off for the English Channel port of Dover with its bow doors still open and, as a result, water had got onto the car deck. If you've ever tried to carry a baking tray with even a shallow covering of water in it, you'll know how unstable a configuration this is. Tragically, the ferry capsized some 30 years ago, becoming one of Britain's worst maritime disasters, as 193 people died, with entire families and groups of friends drowning in freezing waters. For some that day, Andrew Parker would become a life-saver and a hero, by throwing his expansive frame across a gaping chasm down to the cold waters.

Try to keep that incident in mind, please, as you listen to how Paul opens his letter to first century Christians in the Churches of God located in the Roman province known then as Galatia. In particular, listen out for the one who's described as our rescuer.

> "Paul, an apostle (not sent from men nor through the agency of man, but through Jesus Christ and God the Father, who raised Him from the dead), and all the brethren who are with me, To the churches of Galatia: Grace to you and peace from God our Father and the Lord Jesus Christ, who gave Himself for our sins so

> that He might rescue us from this present evil age, according to the will of our God and Father, to whom be the glory forevermore. Amen." (Galatians 1:1-5)

Paul tells us Christ gave himself for our sins so that he might rescue us. In his human body on the cross he bridged over hell's gaping chasm, so that each believer on himself might pass safely from death to life – and from deserved condemnation to unmerited justification – which means us having a right standing before God, with all our sins removed. But Paul says – and I hope you noticed – that Christ rescued us from this present evil age. Not by instantly taking us out of it. No, he leaves us here as his witnesses – in an environment that's hostile to our faith. The prevailing system of thought all around us in the media is influenced by God's adversary who's also our adversary. The Lord's rescue of us provides not only for the future but also for the here and now. We can know his rescuing power every day as we serve the Lord.

What else does Paul say? After his opening greeting, he doesn't follow the usual habit of exchanging news about circumstances. But instead he dives straight in with what's on his heart. And the Gospel was always on Paul's heart. It's as if he can't bring himself to exchange niceties while there's a massive 'elephant in the room' – and that was the case, as he saw it, for some of these Galatian Christians had distorted the Gospel – they'd distorted the Christian message by adding to it. Paul comes straight out with his objection as he continues in verse 6:

> "I am amazed that you are so quickly deserting Him who called you by the grace of Christ, for a different

> gospel; which is really not another; only there are some who are disturbing you and want to distort the gospel of Christ. But even if we, or an angel from heaven, should preach to you a gospel contrary to what we have preached to you, he is to be accursed! As we have said before, so I say again now, if any man is preaching to you a gospel contrary to what you received, he is to be accursed! For am I now seeking the favor of men, or of God? Or am I striving to please men? If I were still trying to please men, I would not be a bond-servant of Christ. For I would have you know, brethren, that the gospel which was preached by me is not according to man" (Galatians 1:6-11).

There is no other Gospel. I read recently of a pastor in the United States Bible Belt who conducted a census of his congregation. He discovered that 78% of them believed someone could go to heaven apart from believing in Christ. That's in contradiction to the biblical Gospel. We need to have the same view of the Gospel as Paul. You might have another coffee, but you won't find another Gospel. There is no other. Any other message is different. But some people were troubling these first century believers. Who were they? It was a class of people often referred to as 'Judaizers.' They were Jews, of course - Jews who seemed to believe the Christian message – but the thing was, they insisted on converts living the way Jews had always lived.

The Judaizers believed the truths other Christians believed. They were right down the line, biblically speaking, concerning Jesus being the Messiah and that he'd died for them on the cross. It might not then have seemed to people as if they were denying the

Gospel. It might even have seemed as if they were improving it, by adding parts from the Old Testament to the New. But as soon as you add anything to grace, you lose grace altogether by totally changing its character. This is the big message of Galatians, so let's pause to picture it clearly. Imagine you're about to drink a glass of clean water, but before you do, someone adds a tiny drop of poison to it. Will you still drink it? It's so close to being pure, right? No, wrong. What difference does such a tiny additional drop make? It means the whole glass of water is now contaminated.

The unique quality of the Gospel is that it doesn't tell us what we must do to please God. It tells us that what Christ has done has already pleased God. And it tells us that God's pleased with us when we fully identify with what Christ has done – without any reliance of a contribution of our own. Knowing that we have God's favour, secured for us by what Christ has done for us through his death, we go on to serve the Lord, working in his power and according to his rules. This is grace-based obedience – and it's very different from any attempts of our own at performance-based legalism.

What's legalism? Let's try to explain. There's usually not much to complain about a legalist's behaviour, the worrying thing is their belief. Right behaviour with wrong belief is a sign of a legalist; whereas, on the other hand, wrong behaviour with right belief is a sign of a hypocrite. But right belief coupled with right behaviour should be the sign of every citizen of Heaven's kingdom. Works-based religion is like a treadmill: it gets you nowhere and it wears you out. Let me say it again: legalism is so different from grace-based obedience. In the scheme of grace, we're not working in our own power according to our own rules to earn God's favour – that's what the legalist tries to do. No, we're working in God's power according to his rules, and we who believe, are already totally assured of his favour.

As Paul told the Galatian believers, we need to be quite certain that the good news of God's grace is free. But, let's be equally clear, it's not cheap. Let's illustrate that to make absolutely sure we've got it. Bible teacher G. Campbell Morgan told of a coalminer who came to him and said, "I would give anything to believe that God would forgive my sins, but I cannot believe that he will forgive them if I just ask him. It is too cheap."

Morgan said, "My dear friend, have you been working today?"

"Yes, I was down in the mine." "How did you get up out of the coal-mine? Did you pay?"

"Of course not. I just got into the cage and was pulled up the shaft right to the top."

"Were you not afraid to entrust yourself to that cage? Was it not too cheap?" Morgan asked. "Oh, no," said the miner, "it was cheap for me, but it cost the company a lot of money to sink the shaft." Suddenly, the truth struck him. What cost him nothing - the offer of salvation - had not come cheap to God. This miner had never thought of the great price God paid in sending his Son to rescue fallen humanity. He realized that all anyone had to do was to 'get into the cage,' as it were, by faith.

The big lesson here in the first chapter of Galatians is that as far as the Gospel is concerned, to add to it, is to subtract from it.

Far from enhancing it, it totally destroys it. The Gospel is free in the sense that Christianity does not say 'do,' but rather it says 'it's done.' God the Father initiated our salvation; God the Son accomplished it; and God the Spirit has revealed it. This is the message which sets us free! It also instructs us how we are to live as believers on the Lord Jesus, as the guaranteed citizens of heaven while we're still living on the earth.

> "For the grace of God has appeared, bringing salvation ... instructing us to deny ungodliness and worldly desires and to live sensibly, righteously and godly in the present age, looking for the blessed hope and the appearing of the glory of our great God and Savior, Christ Jesus, who gave Himself for us to redeem us from every lawless deed, and to purify for Himself a people for His own possession, zealous for good deeds" (Titus 2:12-14).

We've said already that God's free grace isn't cheap. It instructs us to deny worldliness in this present (evil) age. This is the grace brought by our rescuer that we thought about in opening. God does care how we live. The rescue of the cross was also about rescuing us from doing evil deeds as we wait for God's son to come and take us to heaven. He still will come and take each and every believer, but how ashamed we'll be of our miserable ingratitude if we've failed to live here on earth among a pure people all focussed on being God's possession in this world. How can we be part of that? By living through grace to please the Lord by faithfully following his will as taught in the New Testament.

CHAPTER ONE: REVIEW QUESTIONS

1. In what way can we sense we're being rescued from the evils of society around us?
2. In your own experience of sharing the Gospel, what is the most skewed idea you find you have to overcome?
3. Can you give a contemporary example of right behaviour motivated by wrong beliefs?
4. How would you sum up the 'unique selling point' of Christianity?
5. How does the distinction made between Christianity's message being "free but not cheap" bring us back to our starting point of the rescue of the cross in its present sense?

CHAPTER TWO: THE HANDSHAKE (GALATIANS 1:12-2:10)

It's good to shake hands at the settling of any matter. Let me tell you about five men who shook hands. Although it must be said, as is often the case, living up to the terms of the agreement they'd arrived at turned out to be somewhat tricky. That was definitely the case for one of them: he was the Apostle Peter. Peter's propensity to deny truth for the sake of momentary popularity would again let him down – in a sense reminiscent of what had happened at the time of our Lord's arrest and trial (Luke 22:61). We might almost say that Satan had played Peter that way on an even earlier occasion when he'd tried to banish thoughts of the cross from the Lord's mind (Matthew 16:23). Much later, and quite unwittingly, Peter would once again become Satan's instrument in attempting to obscure the Gospel (Galatians 2:11).

But, to be fair, it was no easier for another man who'd shaken hands that same day. His name was Barnabas, another apostle, and one known for his compassionate nature. But soothing the feelings of others by pragmatic negotiation, while sometimes invaluable, would turn out to be a serious misjudgement in this instance (Galatians 2:13). In contrast to those two men, it was in the formerly hostile Rabbi, Saul of Tarsus, that the gospel found its staunchest, most resolute supporter. He was another of those five men who'd shaken hands, but he was one who remained loyal to the terms of the agreement (Galatians 2:9).

There's a fascinating insight into what followed the handshake we've referred to – and it's given by Paul as he writes his circular letter to the New Testament Churches of God in the province then known as Galatia. He begins with some personal touches in the first chapter. Under fire at the time, he seems to need to go out of his way to demonstrate how minimal his contact with the other apostles had been up until then. He tells them – and us - that he'd received the Gospel independently of the others - in fact, directly from the Lord himself. He maintains that the gospel he preached before his most recent contact with the Jerusalem leaders (see Acts 11:30) was exactly the same as he was still preaching. His summary of the private leaders' conference at Jerusalem which had concluded with the afore-mentioned handshake was this: those reckoned to be of repute had neither added to the content of his preaching nor to its authority (Galatians 2:6). In other words, there had been no change necessary, because, of course, his message and his commissioning had come directly from the Lord.

By the time he comes to write Galatians chapter 2, Paul's now a fairly seasoned preacher, having preached in Damascus, then in Tarsus and surrounding Cilicia, and after that he'd been injected into the mission work at Antioch by Barnabas, who had been his early advocate turned recruiter. Antioch was to become Paul's home church, and serve as a bridgehead for the Gentile mission of which he was the leader. Antioch was an exciting place to be back then, ever since the Gospel pioneers from Africa and Cyprus had made landfall there and broken the previous mould of Jews preaching only to Jews (Acts 11:20). Some of the pioneers from northern Africa became, reasonably enough, leaders of the local church at Antioch. Lucius was one of them, and whether he's one and the same as the Gentile doctor Luke who acted like Paul's personal physician, we can't be sure, but it may just be possible (Acts 13:1).

And it's still only a plausible assumption - no more than that - that Simeon, known by the nickname Niger, might also have come from Cyrene in Africa – and might even be one and the same as Simon of Cyrene, otherwise known as the father of Rufus and Alexander, whose wife had acted like a mother to Paul while he was in Antioch (Mark 15:21; Romans 16:13). Paul's later graphic accounts of the crucifixion whenever he preached (Galatians 3:1) could easily have originated in first-hand accounts he obtained in the home of the man who had carried the cross for Jesus.

From Antioch, Paul and Barnabas - or Barnabas and Saul as they were more often referred to back then - were commissioned for their evangelical ministry. That's as maybe, and it's certainly true, but Paul was at pains to stress to the Galatians that it was really the Lord who had commissioned him directly from the beginning, from his time in Damascus and Arabia. This is where he begins to document his primary credentials to the Galatians, as it were. Paul's so keen to demonstrate the authentic message that he preached that he says this at the close of Galatians 1:

> "For I neither received it from man, nor was I taught it, but I received it through a revelation of Jesus Christ. For you have heard of my former manner of life in Judaism, how I used to persecute the church of God beyond measure and tried to destroy it; and

> I was advancing in Judaism beyond many of my contemporaries among my countrymen, being more extremely zealous for my ancestral traditions. But when God, who had set me apart even from my mother's womb and called me through His grace, was pleased to reveal His Son in me so that I might preach Him among the Gentiles, I did not immediately consult with flesh and blood, nor did I go up to Jerusalem to those who were apostles before me; but I went away to Arabia, and returned once more to Damascus.
>
> Then three years later I went up to Jerusalem to become acquainted with Cephas, and stayed with him fifteen days. But I did not see any other of the apostles except James, the Lord's brother. (Now in what I am writing to you, I assure you before God that I am not lying.) Then I went into the regions of Syria and Cilicia. I was still unknown by sight to the churches of Judea which were in Christ; but only, they kept hearing, "He who once persecuted us is now preaching the faith which he once tried to destroy." And they were glorifying God because of me" (Galatians 1:12-23).

Just back to the point we were making before ... notice how Paul has said that after his Damascus road experience he didn't head for Jerusalem and the apostles there, no, he went off into Arabia. In other words, he was alone with the Lord in preparation for his future life of service. While it's not clear if Paul was in Arabia for all, or even most of, the three years that get a mention here, it's still true that this reinforces the point made in the lives of Moses, Elijah, and John the Baptist. And that lesson is the need for extensive preparation.

Following that, he did go to Jerusalem where he spent fifteen days becoming acquainted with Peter (Galatians 1:18; see Acts 9:28). We can only imagine how invaluable, instructive and absorbing such an experience would have been, as Paul learnt from the three years in which Peter had been a close companion of the Lord, one of the inner circle of three whom the Lord occasionally had selected to receive more intimate experiences of his power than the others. In addition to personal preparation, how valuable it is to spend quality time with those who have walked closely with the Lord. Then there was for Paul a period of being 'unknown' in his home territory without 'celebrity status,' but with all the glory for his conversion going to God. We probably do converts with dramatically changed lives a total disservice today when we treat them as some kind of Christian celebrity.

But we need to get back to Paul's letter to the Galatians. Remember he was writing to them in order to clarify the Gospel. I believe it's useful to try to sketch a possible sequence of events. We'll start with the early verses of Galatians 2:

> "Then after an interval of fourteen years I went up again to Jerusalem with Barnabas, taking Titus along also. It was because of a revelation that I went up; and I submitted to them the gospel which I preach among the Gentiles, but I did so in private to those who

> were of reputation, for fear that I might be running, or had run, in vain. But not even Titus, who was with me, though he was a Greek, was compelled to be circumcised. But it was because of the false brethren secretly brought in, who had sneaked in to spy out our liberty which we have in Christ Jesus, in order to bring us into bondage.
>
> But we did not yield in subjection to them for even an hour, so that the truth of the gospel would remain with you. But from those who were of high reputation (what they were makes no difference to me; God shows no partiality) - well, those who were of reputation contributed nothing to me. But on the contrary, seeing that I had been entrusted with the gospel to the uncircumcised, just as Peter had been to the circumcised (for He who effectually worked for Peter in his apostleship to the circumcised effectually worked for me also to the Gentiles), and recognizing the grace that had been given to me, James and Cephas and John, who were reputed to be pillars, gave to me and Barnabas the right hand of fellowship, so that we might go to the Gentiles and they to the circumcised. They only asked us to remember the poor - the very thing I also was eager to do" (Galatians 2:1-10).

Before this private conference in Jerusalem (Galatians 2:2; see Acts 11:30), Peter had been given his own revelation of God's purpose as it involved Gentiles. He'd been instrumental in the conversion of Cornelius and reported back and pacified the zealous Jews in Jerusalem (Acts 10 & 11). About the same time, Barnabas had been commissioned to check out reports of Gospel progress among Gentiles at Antioch, and he'd soon brought Paul into the fray there (Acts 11:20-26). It would seem that Peter and Paul were on the same page at this point, and the mother church at Jerusalem, which was increasingly under James' leadership, was altogether comfortable with that. At the private conference, when the five had shaken hands, they'd drawn up lines of demarcation: Peter would focus on the conversion of Jews and Paul on the conversion of Gentiles (Galatians 2:7). But practically every city in the world of the eastern Mediterranean had mixed populations of Jews and Gentiles, so the lines were bound to get crossed. Also, at that private conference, the issue of circumcision didn't seem to have been a major discussion point – as witness the fact that there had been no pressure on Titus, a Greek, to become circumcised. Things were soon to change, however, as we'll see, with early Christian harmony soon to be tested.

CHAPTER TWO: REVIEW QUESTIONS

1. Peter, like any of us, was susceptible to pressure. When is it right to build consensus and when should we commit to a more unpopular line?
2. What, do you think, was the importance of Paul being commissioned independently of the other Apostles?
3. What are some features of Paul's life before his 'breakthrough' into being used as God's 'chosen vessel' that commend themselves as helpful character formation?
4. Would you like to conjecture on how the different personalities converging in the church at Antioch, and its pioneer character, might have helped shape the greatest missionary ever?

CHAPTER THREE: TROUBLE BACK AT BASE (GALATIANS 2:11-2:21)

As the ship nosed into the mouth of the Orontes river, it was bringing back Paul and Barnabas from a successful missionary enterprise which had seen them reach as far as Derbe. The Church of God at Antioch in Syria was now a mother church in its own right, for now there were daughter churches planted in the hinterlands of the northern Mediterranean shoreline. But it had been far from plain sailing. There had been confrontation with orthodox Jewish communities in places like Iconium; and they'd received mistaken adulation from pagans during cross-cultural miscommunication at Lystra; and, what's more, Paul had made a shock arrival at Derbe after being presumed dead following a stoning incident. According to scholars and historians (see F.F. Bruce, Paul Apostle of the Free Spirit, p.172), that last city was a frontier city of the Roman province of Galatia (at one time anyway). As was often his custom, Paul lost no time writing to the new churches of Galatia, being anxious that they should stand fast in their new-found faith.

And, indeed, there was no time to lose. We're told Paul spent a long time with the mother church at Antioch at this stage (Acts 14:28). I'm sure there was the thrill of giving them mission reports, but soon, if not from the outset, those reports became mingled with concern for the stability of the Galatian churches. And the mother church itself was gripped with the same issue that troubled the daughter churches.

The Jewish rite of circumcision was fast becoming a major cause of dissension in places where both Jews and Gentiles were turning to Christ. What had brought this about? For years, perhaps, the Gospel had been spreading in Antioch without this matter of circumcision previously being such a major issue. In Caesarea, when Peter had preached to Cornelius and family there had been no mention of it being controversial there either. However, around the time of Paul's first missionary journey, as the Gospel penetrated further into modern day Turkey, the peace was being disturbed back at the Antioch base. We can assume this was the first mission launched from Antioch, and not from Jerusalem, and so when reports began circulating back of a rapid intake of Gentile believers into the expanding community of the Christian Faith, some in the church at Jerusalem may have become concerned. After all, converted pagans might easily let the side down! How could they be expected to reach an ethical standard of lifestyle?

It might also be worth asking what'd been happening politically in Jerusalem between Acts chapters 11 and 15 - for those who were now troubling the churches in Turkey and Syria had come from there. Well, there had been the sudden death of Herod Agrippa (see the end of Acts 12), in turn followed by various Jewish uprisings against the return to a more direct form of Roman rule. Supporters of these uprisings would inevitably be suspicious of any Roman collaborators. And it's possible that Christian Jews who had links with those building bridges to the Gentile world might be thought to belong in that category. It's possible then that Gospel expansion into Asia Minor posed political problems back in 'the old country' which had been

Christianity's cradle. Those whose agenda was shaped as much by political as by ethical concerns perhaps saw the imposition of circumcision as going some way to solving this problem. Not only did it symbolize the ethical commitment, but it might prove unattractive to Gentiles, which would ease the political pressure by limiting their numbers.

Matters soon came to a showdown at Antioch. The Apostle Peter came to visit. That in itself wasn't a problem, of course. He'd learned at first-hand from the Lord that it was perfectly permissible for him to eat with Gentiles (Acts 10:9-19). He'd also previously at Jerusalem shaken hands with Paul on the understanding that there was no need for Gentile Christians to be circumcised or live like Jews (Galatians 2:3). All this meant that Peter had mingled freely with Gentiles at Antioch until certain Jerusalem-based men had arrived there, having come from James, the Lord's brother – although it's unlikely they'd been authorized by him (Acts 15). Let's pick up Paul's version of events ...

> "But when Cephas came to Antioch, I opposed him to his face, because he stood condemned. For prior to the coming of certain men from James, he used to eat with the Gentiles; but when they came, he began to withdraw and hold himself aloof, fearing the party of the circumcision. The rest of the Jews joined him in hypocrisy, with the result that even Barnabas was carried away by their hypocrisy. But when I saw that they were not straightforward about the truth of the gospel, I said to Cephas in the presence of all, "If you, being a Jew, live like the Gentiles and not like the

> Jews, how is it that you compel the Gentiles to live like Jews?" (Galatians 2:11-14).

When those pushing such an agenda arrived at Antioch, Peter was already there. Under pressure, Peter stopped behaving in accordance with his convictions – and the previously mentioned handshake – and he ceased to have meals with Gentile believers. Paul charged Peter with hypocrisy or 'play-acting' simply because this was not the behaviour he'd signed up to. Peter was truly no Judaizer, so why was he acting the part of one? He wouldn't be the last preacher to modify his message to suit his audience. Paul now proceeds to nail the doctrine. Luther would later make famous the term 'justification by faith.' Summing it up to the Galatian Christians in his letter to them, Paul says:

> "We are Jews by nature and not sinners from among the Gentiles; nevertheless knowing that a man is not justified by the works of the Law but through faith in Christ Jesus, even we have believed in Christ Jesus, so that we may be justified by faith in Christ and not by the works of the Law; since by the works of the Law no flesh will be justified" (Galatians 2:15-16).

Paul set things straight at Antioch, correcting Peter and doubtless, Barnabas. But after writing to the Galatia churches, Paul and Barnabas would set out for Jerusalem to settle the same issue there once and for all and to prevent a different Gospel which could never be a true alternative. The landmark Jerusalem Council decision of Acts 15 would set the benchmark for all time, to which Reformers like Luther, as we say, would return much later. In effect, Paul says there's never been one single person born of a human father in all the history of our planet who has made himself acceptable to God based on performing religious good works.

Verse 16 says very plainly "we have believed in Christ Jesus, so that we may be justified." The theology of justification by faith is biblically unassailable. But are the works of the law as mentioned in this verse being contrasted with our faith placed objectively in Christ; or are the works of the law in this verse set over against the faithfulness of Christ himself? I had never considered the second possibility until it surfaced recently over a mug of coffee at one of our Charity Coffee Mornings, but it's a translation that can be defended and is even arguably better. It was the translation choice made by the translators of the King James version. It's certainly by believing in Christ that we are justified, and the first part of the verse says that very clearly, but here's the question: 'Is this justification - which is not brought about by the works of the law – is it further taught here to be the result of the faithfulness of Christ?' The next part of the verse literally reads: 'justified by the faith(fulness) of Christ.' Viewed in this way, the faithfulness of Christ becomes a contrasting theme of the letter Paul wrote to the Galatians. His faithfulness in rescuing us from this present evil age; his faithfulness in coming as the ultimate fulfilment of the promise to Abraham which pre-dated even the law; and his faithfulness in coming at the precise time to be born of a woman and under the law so as to bring us out from under its condemnation. This would be a fitting rejoinder to the Judaizers.

And there's another example of the faithfulness of Christ which we'll come to now as we conclude our reading of Galatians chapter two:

> "But if, while seeking to be justified in Christ, we ourselves have also been found sinners, is Christ then a minister of sin? May it never be! For if I rebuild what I have once destroyed, I prove myself to be a transgressor. For through the Law I died to the Law, so that I might live to God. I have been crucified with Christ; and it is no longer I who live, but Christ lives in me; and the life which I now live in the flesh I live by faith in the Son of God, who loved me and gave Himself up for me. I do not nullify the grace of God, for if righteousness comes through the Law, then Christ died needlessly" (Galatians 2:17-21).

Paul writes of how as a believer in Christ's death for his sins on the cross, he'd died to the penalty of the law. This had happened in the death of Christ. In God's judicial reckoning he'd died with Christ to the penalty of the law. Now every born-again Christian believer can say with Paul that Christ lives in him or her - and indeed that their experience of human life now is one of living by the faithfulness of the Son of God. It would seem that it's this rendering which explains most adequately the ending of that famous personal verse of Christian testimony. For the faithfulness of Christ is supremely demonstrated in the faithful love that led him to give himself up sacrificially for each one who believes in him. Having received him as personal saviour, the believer knows as a result, of course, that he or she is declared righteous before God.

CHAPTER THREE: REVIEW QUESTIONS

1. Having rehearsed, in brief, the encounters Paul had experienced in evangelism, what are your most memorable experiences?
2. It's heart-breaking when new converts are sidetracked into error. Which Old Testament elements today are the most likely contenders for addition to New Testament faith?
3. It's conceivable that politics back then played a role in some measure in attempting to shape the content of Christian faith. What undue influence might parallel this today?
4. Discuss why Paul chose to accuse Peter of hypocrisy, not heresy.
5. If we split v.16 into 4 parts, a-d, based on the above (NASB) punctuation, then 'justification by (our) faith (in Christ)' is already clear from parts a & b. Do you think v.16c is repeating the same or saying something different?

CHAPTER FOUR: IT ALL POINTS TO FAITH ALONE (GALATIANS 3)

The migration of people is very much a topical concern. But, of course, it's not new. One theory on migration of ancient people and language groups, holds that long ago a group of people, variously known as the Celts or the Gauls, migrated westwards as far as the British Isles and eastwards through the Balkans into a central portion of modern-day Turkey. This third century BC expansion left a pocket of Gauls in what was then Asia Minor, and known to New Testament readers as Galatia. This ethnic Galatia was smaller than the province the Romans called Galatia which extended to the south and included the cities mentioned in Acts chapter 14. It was to them, of course, the Apostle Paul wrote a Bible letter.

Some writers, outside of the Bible (Callimachus & Hillary, see Barnes), have written disparagingly of the Gauls, but when the Apostle Paul begins his third chapter by describing them as 'foolish,' he probably wasn't intending a national slight. But he didn't hesitate from using such language to describe the Galatian Christians. He literally called them 'lacking in understanding.' Of special concern was their instability. Paul reminds them how he'd placarded Christ before them in his preaching, but somehow they had allowed the Judaizers to come along - and it was almost as if they'd given them the evil eye or bewitched them. They had moved away from the biblical Gospel of 'faith alone in Christ alone by grace alone.' As someone might add a drop of poison to water, these false teachers had added aspects of law observance to their pure faith.

Paul at once demands to know if they'd received God's Holy Spirit as a result of recently placing their faith in Christ as personal saviour or had they received the Spirt while obeying the works of the law? (In fact, he asks them six rapid-fire questions in the first 5 verses). For a second time, he scolds them for their foolish lack of understanding (v.3). The answer to this incisive question should've been so blindingly obvious. Like a teacher helping students work through a live tutorial session, he guides them to the answer which he delivers in verse 14: "we ... receive the promise of the Spirit through faith." But his way of arriving at the answer is instructive as it majors on the great ancestral figure of Abraham.

It's worth us all weighing up the strength of the Apostle's arguments, because in every generation there's a danger which spreads in from the cults – and it's essentially the same danger which was faced down in the first century – it's the danger of reverting to works in some form or another. Today, you hear some groups saying you need to observe the sabbath or you need to be baptized and pay tithes. The general form is always the same – it's always faith plus something in order to be saved and stay saved. The particular issue in Paul's time for Jewish Christians was circumcision. They even wanted Gentiles who came to faith in Christ to be circumcised. Of course, they could rightly say: 'but it says it in the Bible!' What they didn't – and some today don't - appreciate is that the Bible's revelation is progressive. Beginning with God's restart with Abraham, and leading on through the time of the Law given through Moses,

Paul is now going to show them the final and fullest revelation of God in Christ.

It was very relevant that Paul by the Spirit first singled out Abraham. Pagan Abraham (Joshua 24) had done nothing to merit the privilege of being called by God (Acts 7:2-5; Genesis 12). God's dealings are always about grace. Grace on God's part; and faith to receive it on our part. And for Abraham it would be a radical faith which required a man nearing 100, and with no children, to believe that he'd become – on the basis of God's word alone – the father of a great nation, a nation which would in turn be the means of bringing blessing into all the world. God didn't give Abraham a single square meter of real estate but gave him his word, his promise for the future. God's promise to Abraham showed the necessity of faith. Genuine faith is expressed in radical obedience.

Abraham is a significant choice in Paul's argument for yet another reason because he was the first man God ever commanded to be circumcised (Genesis 17:9-14). The major point in Paul's reasoning is that Abraham was regarded as righteous in God's sight before his circumcision. His right status with God was not down to his having been circumcised – far less was it about his law observance for the law wouldn't arrive for another 400 years! Listen to Paul on the same topic, but this time when writing to Christians in Rome:

> "BLESSED IS THE MAN WHOSE SIN THE LORD WILL NOT TAKE INTO ACCOUNT."

> Is this blessing then on the circumcised, or on the uncircumcised also? For we say, "FAITH WAS CREDITED TO ABRAHAM AS RIGHTEOUSNESS." How then was it credited? While he was circumcised, or uncircumcised? Not while circumcised, but while uncircumcised; and he received the sign of circumcision, a seal of the righteousness of the faith which he had while uncircumcised, so that he might be the father of all who believe without being circumcised, that righteousness might be credited to them" (Romans 4:8-11).

It's unmistakable in God's Word, isn't it? Abraham was credited as being right with God before he was ever circumcised. Back in Galatians chapter 3 again: "Now that no one is justified by the Law before God is evident; for, "THE RIGHTEOUS MAN SHALL LIVE BY FAITH" (Galatians 3:11). Some will recognize this as Luther's verse, quoted here by Paul from Habakkuk 2:4. Galatians, Romans, now Habakkuk, blending together to show the unwavering consistency of the Bible – in this case as it bears upon the basic truth of the Christian message. As well as telling us that faith like Abraham's faith brings blessing; Paul also says that the Law brings a curse through our inability to keep it. Then comes the good news in Galatians 3:13: "Christ redeemed us from the curse of the Law, having become a curse for us - for it is written, "CURSED IS EVERYONE WHO HANGS ON A TREE."

Remarkably, this actual quotation comes from Deuteronomy chapter 21 where it relates most closely to the case of disobedient sons who had committed misdemeanours worthy of death. They were strung up, regarded as objects accursed by God. The Apostle Paul applies it to Christ on the cross. Striking contrast, isn't it? He is God's son, fully obedient, but entering in under God's curse in our place and on account of our disobedience.

Well, these thoughts bring Paul to Moses, and Paul begins to deal with the law and its proper place in God's purposes. The law was given to show that humanity is sinful at the core, chronically disobeying the law of God, and in need of salvation. The law doesn't make us sinners, but it exposes our sin. It's aptly described in this role as being like a tutor giving instructions to children. Luther said the law's design is to make men worse not better. We discover we need grace because we stand cursed beneath the law. With Abraham it was all about blessing; with Moses, the curses became prominent (see Deuteronomy 27:26). We need to get things the right way round. Successively, in the third chapter of Galatians, we explore with Paul 1) the necessity of faith; 2) the futility of our own fallen flesh; and 3) the freedom that's alone found in Christ. As God shaped history, everything was building to this: that the promise given at the first to Abraham pinpointed the Christ who was coming (v.16). The Law, also, was given until the coming of Christ (v.24), the one to whom it was designed to lead us. The whole of the Old Testament, including the Law, was saying 'look to Christ.' He was the one to obey the Law for us, and also bear its curse for us. Jesus takes the curse and completes the promise.

I was speaking the other day to a fine Christian man who appeared to think that persons in the Old Testament were not saved by faith because they lived before the cross – we spoke of how they didn't realize all the details of what God would do in Christ, but their faith was still in the Gospel (v.8) – Abraham's Gospel! Salvation has always been by faith. The danger of ignoring the Old Testament is to enslave ourselves again – for the Law prepares us for grace! The study of the Old Testament law shouldn't be ignored by us, for its importance lies in us seeing that it firstly was like a prison where we're convicted of our sin; and secondly was like a personal tutor to bring us to Jesus Christ, the great liberator. It's the faithfulness of Christ (Galatians 3:23-26) that has made the difference: freeing us, justifying us and adopting us as sons of God.

Paul's been talking about Jewish believers having the status of mere minors during their Judaism phase. Their status was much the same as that of a household slave whose education was being supervised by a family employee. Paul says, when the faithfulness of Christ was manifested, as promised before the Law was given, those same Jewish believers finally attained their majority status. Things suddenly changed with their faith in Christ. I was particularly struck with how their water baptism is referred to. Of course, it's only the symbol of their faith, but the text tells us that this was when they "clothed themselves with Christ" (Galatians 3:27). That's a striking expression: 'to clothe oneself with Christ.' This would be like when a youth in that Roman society got his garment of manhood (toga virilis). Spiritually then, a believer's baptism is signifying he or she has come of age by the hearing of faith, which was what the prior tutelage under the Law had been designed by God to prepare them for.

So, what's the practical impact of this colourful language? An early Christian commentator put it like this: "He who is clothed appears to be that with which he is clothed." The stand we take in baptism should coincide with our active attempt to appear to behave like Christ. Saved through faith alone in Christ alone, and freed to live to please God, we express our dedication in the waters of believers' baptism by total immersion.

CHAPTER FOUR: REVIEW QUESTIONS

1. Paul assumed it was obvious to them that they had the Spirit. When and how has his residence within you, a believer, been obvious to you? Which Bible verses clinches it for you?
2. What type of preaching (content) today might lead us to take our eyes off the cross?
3. Why should Christians read the Old Testament?
4. Put in your own words the progression of revelation that Paul walks us through in Galatians chapter 3.
5. Do the previous examples of Abraham and Moses (implicitly) point again to the emphasis being on Christ's own faithfulness here? If so, where?

CHAPTER FIVE: THE FAITHFULNESS OF CHRIST (GALATIANS 4: 1-10)

Paul's been talking about Jewish believers having the status of mere minors during their Judaism phase of existence: and by that we mean while they served God under the Law given through Moses until Christ came. It's during that gap - from Moses to Christ - that they were considered minors. This means that their status back then was comparable with that of a household slave whose education was being supervised by a family employee. But it was always in God's overall plan that the Law should be given before Christ came. In chapters 3 and 4 of Galatians, we read about God giving his promise to Abraham; then giving his Law through Moses; and then giving His son, Jesus; and finally, he gave his Holy Spirit to reside in all New Testament believers in Christ. This is the orderly, planned giving of a truly great Giver!

Today, the study of the Old Testament law shouldn't be ignored by Christians, for although it's now fulfilled in Christ (Matthew 5:17), its importance lies in us seeing that it always was like a prison where all of humanity lay convicted of sin; and secondly, it was always envisaged as being like a personal tutor to bring people to Jesus, the great liberator from that prison where all are trapped by their own sin.

In working our way through Galatians, we've been picking up Paul's emphasis on the faithfulness of Christ, God's son. How wonderful to see it set out so fully that it's the faithfulness of Christ (Galatians 3:23-26) that's made all the difference: freeing us, justifying us and adopting us as sons to God. Let's now hear what Paul says as we begin chapter 4 of Galatians:

> "Now I say, as long as the heir is a child, he does not differ at all from a slave although he is owner of everything, but he is under guardians and managers until the date set by the father. So also we, while we were children, were held in bondage under the elemental things of the world. But when the fullness of the time came, God sent forth His Son, born of a woman, born under the Law, so that He might redeem those who were under the Law, that we might receive the adoption as sons. Because you are sons, God has sent forth the Spirit of His Son into our hearts, crying, "Abba! Father!"
>
> Therefore you are no longer a slave, but a son; and if a son, then an heir through God. However at that time, when you did not know God, you were slaves to those which by nature are no gods. But now that you have come to know God, or rather to be known by God, how is it that you turn back again to the weak and worthless elemental things, to which you desire to be enslaved all over again? You observe days and months and seasons and years" (Galatians 4:1-10).

Paul informs us that when the faithfulness of Christ was manifested, as had been promised before the Law was given, Jewish Christian believers finally attained their majority status. They came of age, as it were, with the granting of full sonship through adoption. As we move into chapter 4 of Galatians, Paul maintains the theme of how believers become sons of God – with our adoption having past, present and future implications.

Before going on to mention more about the believer's adoption, it may be as well to make a comment about Paul's reference to 'elemental things' which was repeated in that Bible section we've just cited from the top of Galatians chapter 4. Bible scholar, F.F. Bruce (in Paul, Apostle of the Free Spirit), makes the suggestion that this might have been a reference to celestial bodies. Throughout history, pagans often worshipped objects in the heavens: the stars and planets seen in the night sky. Bruce suggests it was, in one sense, even possible for monotheistic Jews to return to that – but that would be true only in the sense that these objects lay behind the defining of the days, months, seasons and years which they tended to hold in too high an esteem.

Be that as it may, we want now to explore what the Bible says here about our adoption in a spiritual sense. We've already seen that we're all sons of God through faith (Galatians 3:26); and the Bible here has informed us that each believer on Christ has received the Spirit of adoption – a reference to God's Holy Spirit who indwells us as the Spirit of adoption from the moment we put trust in Christ for eternal salvation (Romans 8:15). Among the wonderful blessings our salvation has brought us is the fact that we've been placed in the unalterable position of being joint heirs with Christ (Romans 8:17). We are for ever those who have been adopted as sons to God through Jesus Christ (Ephesians 1:3,11,14). That placing as sons, as we say, took place at our conversion, and so it's in our past.

But Paul also deals with our present experience as believers. Remember, only Paul uses this word 'adoption' in the New Testament Scriptures. And in Romans 8:14, he says "As many as are led by the Spirit are sons of God." At first this seems to be saying that we need to know the Holy Spirit's leading daily in our lives for us to qualify as sons of God. But when we compare scripture with scripture, and recall Galatians 3:26 which says we are "all sons of God through faith," we realize that can't be right. All believers are sons of God by virtue of the faithfulness of Christ (Galatians 3:22-26). All of us who believe in Christ alone for salvation are children of God by birth - the new birth - and we're equally sons of God by adoption. And if we live by the Spirit, what happens is we actually make it plain in our lives that we're sons of God. If we're Spirit-led in what we say and do in serving the Lord, it's obvious to those around us that we're sons of God.

That leads us into considering our lives of service for God in a bit more biblical detail. If we take the Church of God at Corinth, we find Paul applying one of God's Old Testament commands in Second Corinthians chapter 6 when he says: "... be separate and ... be to me sons" (2 Corinthians 6:14-18). It seems this is another case of the Spirit of God appealing to believers 'to become what they are.' This is an interesting quote – at least it appears to be a quotation from the second book of Samuel chapter 7 verse 14 when the prophet Nathan came to King David – after he'd expressed a desire to build a temple, a house on earth for the God of heaven. Through Nathan, God says to David: "I will raise up your descendant after you ... I will establish his kingdom ... he shall build a house for My name ... I will be a father to him and he will be a son to Me."

We know that God regarded the whole of Israel as his son. He declared through Moses to Pharaoh "Israel is My son, My firstborn" (Exodus 4:22; see also Hosea 11:1). But here – and all bound up with the idea of the building of God's house – God reinforces the thought of sonship specifically for Solomon, the king of David's dynasty or royal line. By carrying out God's purpose in the building of his earthly house, Solomon would characterize and give full expression to the special relationship God intended all Israel to enjoy. So he's affirmed as **being** a son to God.

Notice the force of the word 'being' – he will be a son to Me, God said. Imagine a human family where the father is never at home. A son growing up in that family might find a role model in some other adult male figure. If this proved to be a good influence, others might even say 'that man is more of a father to him than his real father.' There's such a thing as acting in a way that's consistent with what we are. In that sense, 'being a son to God' carries us into the idea of our behaviour being exactly what it should be for those who already are sons of God.

And, remember, that's precisely what God says through Paul to those in the Church of God at Corinth: "you shall **be** sons and daughters to Me." Notice how the context in the New Testament agrees fully with the Old Testament context in terms of the building of God's house. 'How is that?' you ask. Well, remember Paul's writing to the Church of God at Corinth, and in 1 Corinthians 3:9, he's described them as 'God's building' when calling on each in the church to be careful how he or she builds. So, once again it's God's people who are being addressed, and it's about building for God in the house of God, which is the Bible-wide theme that lies close to God's heart; a theme that goes beyond our salvation and into the realm of our lives of service for God. To have a place in God's house, demands of us that God's requirements are met. Just as all Israel could be regarded as God's son, but the one among them who fulfilled God's will fully in building a house for God was singled out as being a son to God; so today all believers on the Lord Jesus are sons of God through faith, but we demonstrate our sonship best by active service in relation to serving God's will in God's house.

And what does the future hold for us as sons of God? To discover more, we need to come back again to Romans chapter 8 – let's read from verse 19 to get the full sense:

> "For the anxious longing of the creation waits eagerly for the revealing of the sons of God. For the creation was subjected to futility, not willingly, but because of Him who subjected it, in hope that the creation itself also will be set free from its slavery to corruption into the freedom of the glory of the children of God. For we know that the whole creation groans and suffers the pains of childbirth together until now. And not only this, but also we ourselves, having the first fruits of the Spirit, even we ourselves groan within ourselves, waiting eagerly for our adoption as sons, the redemption of our body" (Romans 8:19-23).

Paul begins by mentioning the 'anxious longing' of creation as it eagerly awaits the revealing of the sons of God. Those eagerly awaited future events, when the sons of God are to be revealed, begin with the change in the physical bodies of all believers at the return of Christ for the Church which is His Body. As Paul says in 1 Thessalonians 4, at that time the dead in Christ will rise and we who remain alive then will be changed and caught up together with them to meet our Lord in the air. What a glorious moment that'll be! Our adoption then will be complete in every sense: our physical bodies then reflecting our status as sons of God. As Paul says, we wait eagerly for this.

CHAPTER FIVE: REVIEW QUESTIONS

1. Another suggestion for 'elemental spirits' is that this was a reference to angelic beings through whose agency the Law was ordained (Galatians 3:19) and to whom too much respect for attributed for this. Any thoughts?
2. How is God shown to be the great Giver in this section of the letter?
3. Do you think we are adopted sons of God by our faith or through the faithfulness of Christ – or is it both? Explain your answer.
4. How do we make it obvious what we already are (as sons)?
5. If we teach salvation in 3 aspects or tenses (from sin's penalty, power & presence); can you sum up adoption in much the same way?

CHAPTER SIX: THE FORMATION OF CHRIST (GALATIANS 4:11-20)

Adoption back in New Testament times was often an adoption of adults, and even at times, of slaves. Careful selection was done, all with the goal in mind that the person being adopted would be someone who could be trusted to enhance the family reputation. We should be aware of the fact that, in Roman times, a father had near absolute legal authority over his children (*patria potestas*). This extended to the power of life and death over them, and it continued as long as the father remained alive - no matter the age of the child. Children were more or less viewed as possessions.

This meant that whenever a Roman man of wealth and prominence wanted to adopt a young man, the absolute power of the birth father over the son had to be transferred to him, that is to the father who was doing the adopting. How this happened was through an elaborate process in which the birth father would first symbolically sell and then buy back his son twice, but after selling him a third time he didn't buy him back again – what this achieved was that it symbolized the breaking of his ownership rights, and the transfer of that absolute power from the birth father to the new father. In a second step, the adopting father went to a Roman magistrate and presented the legal case for the complete transfer of the rights of the son from his birth father to himself, the adopting father. This was a formal legal transaction for which there were witnesses, as in a court of law.

So, we see, that this ancient adoption process had a distinctly commercial aspect to it: the adopted son was bought out of his old family leaving all his debts and obligations behind him. None of these debts followed him. It was as if his old persona became extinct, and this was a totally new start. The adopted person lost all his rights to his old family, and he gained all the rights of a fully legitimate son in his new family. In the most literal sense, and in the most legally binding way, he got a new father!

In law, the old life of the adopted person was completely wiped out. For example, all debts were legally cancelled; they were wiped out as though they'd never been. The adopted person was regarded as a new person entering into a new life with which the past no longer had anything to do. In the eyes of the law, the adopted person was literally and absolutely the son of the new father. He became heir to his new father's estate. Even if other sons were born afterwards - who were the new father's own flesh and blood - it didn't affect the adopted son's rights in any way, shape or form. Nothing, absolutely nothing, could change the legal fact that he was a co-heir with them.

How well all this illustrates Bible teaching for believers on the Lord Jesus Christ! We, who are all sons of God through faith (Galatians 3:26), have been bought with a price. We've previously read from Galatians chapter 4: "But when the fullness of the time came, God sent forth His Son, born of a woman, born under the Law, so that He might redeem those who were under the Law, that we might receive the adoption as sons" (Galatians 4:4-5).

What we're told, among other things there, is that God sent his son, born to Mary on earth as Jesus Christ, that we might be redeemed from sin's curse, and as a result, be adopted as sons to God through our faith in Jesus Christ. The redemption – which means we were bought back to God – was necessary for this adoption to become a reality. This reminds us of how, in the Roman custom of adoption, the new father bought the son he wished to adopt. There was a commercial basis for the legal transaction of adoption – one which bought out all the debts and obligations of his or her old life – and the adoptee was in reality a new person with a new identity and a new life in the eyes of the law and society then. That's the background to understanding what's happened to the believer on the Lord Jesus.

In those ancient times, adoption was as much - if not more - for the advantage of the family who were doing the adopting. To take a not untypical case: suppose we imagine a family where the natural children are not showing themselves particularly capable of continuing the family business. The head of the household in that case might well look to adopt his most trusted slave who has shown himself to have expert business skills. In this way, the family's future success and reputation could be enhanced by such a strategic move. And is there not a voice for us in that too? But only in this sense: that God has adopted us to carry on his work on earth, and to advance his kingdom.

God has selected us for adoption so that we might be to the praise of his glory. Let's read more about the kind intention of God's will in adopting us from Galatians chapter 4:19: "My children, with whom I am again in labor until Christ is formed in you ..."

God's desire is that he should see his son in the life of everyone he adopts. I want to lay alongside this an Old Testament verse, if I may. It's Isaiah 42:14 which says: "like a woman in labor I will groan" – and this is God speaking! – "I will both gasp and pant." What's this all about? In surrounding sections of the book of the prophet Isaiah, God addresses Israel, and her Messiah, alternately, as being his chosen servant, through whom he'd achieve his ultimate purposes in this world and in the world to come. However, unlike her Messiah, Israel as a nation had a chequered history with variable performance. To get Israel back on track, God at times speaks of being proactive towards them under the figure of a heroic warrior (e.g. Isaiah 42:13). But at other times, the picture radically changes – to that of a pregnant woman, no less!

Like Joseph before his brothers, God, too, had restrained himself – with age-long if not 'eternal' restraint, waiting for the time when Israel would finally rise to her obligations. But later, like a pregnant woman taking deep breaths before the final push, he spoke of putting off restraint - he could wait no longer - and like a woman whose time to give birth has come, he just wanted to get it over with; and so spoke of groaning, gasping and panting.

What remarkable language! We'd never have dared to picture God by analogy with a pregnant woman. How expressive of how God waited with intense longing for his expectation for Israel to be fulfilled.

Remember, it was Paul's turn of phrase in Galatians 4:19 that drew our attention to this. In that verse, Paul said to the Galatian Christians that he was in labour until Christ should be formed in them. Without doubt, these same longings of the Apostle Paul were in a true sense the longings of God himself. And what's more, since our circumstances match those of these first century Christians in all the relevant particulars, we know that this is also God's expectation of us too. He has adopted us to the end that we should bear a family resemblance to his son! By this we mean we're destined to become Christ-like. And God can't wait for that to happen!

There's a golden chain in Roman chapter 8 (v.29) which could be described as having four golden links which span from eternity to eternity and completely sums up God's purpose for us as believers on the Lord Jesus Christ. This is the most wonderful curriculum vitae that anyone could have, qualifying us for an eternity spent with God. It comes down to four words: we're chosen; called; justified and glorified. The last of these has not yet actually taken place, but it is so certain – so bolted-on, rock-solid – that the Holy Spirit caused Paul to use the (aorist!) past tense for a yet future action! That alone should convince everyone about our eternal security in Christ, with no falling away from salvation possible at all.

No-one can fall out anywhere between predestination and glorification. So, even in the analogy with Roman adoption law, it's shown that an adopted son having been placed as a joint-heir with other natural sons could never have his status successfully challenged. His adoption could never be unstitched. It was binding. How much more so, when God speaks, and gives us his word!

Some might wonder why that four-word summary that defines our origin, purpose and destiny doesn't explicitly include the word 'sanctification.' That's because our ultimate sanctification is included in our glorification. We will be glorified with Christ (Romans 8:17). And as 2 Thessalonians 1:10 shows, it's two-way: not only are we to be glorified in him, but he in us! The Lord Jesus was glorified in his physical body while on the mount of Transfiguration (Matthew 17), but he will also be glorified eternally in his mystical spiritual body – which is the Church, all who have put saving faith in the Man of Calvary. Our destiny is to become as Christ-like as it's possible for a creature to become. As near and dear to God as Christ himself is. And God can't wait! Frankly, neither can I!

CHAPTER SIX: REVIEW QUESTIONS

1. What differences can you identify between the practice of adoption in Roman and modern worlds?
2. Attempt to summarize all the ways in which this procedure back then was an almost tailor-made analogy for our spiritual experience.
3. It was often the case then that it was not so much what the family could do for the adoptee, but rather what s/he could do for the new family. How can you advance your heavenly Father's business?
4. Do you think the referred to analogy Isaiah that uses is the Bible's strangest concerning God? If not, which other is? How does Paul suggest we emulate it?
5. Which four words would you choose to describe yourself by?

CHAPTER SEVEN: JERUSALEM ABOVE AS OUR MOTHER (GALATIANS 4:21-31)

Before we leave the fourth chapter of Galatians, I want us to explore its fascinating finale. What we learn from here is something more usually associated with the closing chapters of the letter to the Hebrews. But the Apostle Paul enlists the help of the same New Testament teaching here to emphatically underline the end of legalism and in fact the end of all ritual observance of the Law of Moses by Christians - even in a single part, such as Sabbath observance or avoiding pork or demanding tithes. Here's what Paul has to say:

> "Tell me, you who want to be under law, do you not listen to the law? For it is written that Abraham had two sons, one by the bondwoman and one by the free woman. But the son by the bondwoman was born according to the flesh, and the son by the free woman through the promise. This is allegorically speaking, for these women are two covenants: one proceeding from Mount Sinai bearing children who are to be slaves; she is Hagar. Now this Hagar is Mount Sinai in Arabia and corresponds to the present Jerusalem, for she is in slavery with her children. But the Jerusalem above is free; she is our mother. For it is written, "REJOICE, BARREN WOMAN WHO DOES NOT BEAR; BREAK FORTH AND SHOUT, YOU WHO ARE NOT IN LABOR; FOR MORE

> NUMEROUS ARE THE CHILDREN OF THE DESOLATE THAN OF THE ONE WHO HAS A HUSBAND."
>
> And you brethren, like Isaac, are children of promise. But as at that time he who was born according to the flesh persecuted him who was born according to the Spirit, so it is now also. But what does the Scripture say? "CAST OUT THE BONDWOMAN AND HER SON, FOR THE SON OF THE BONDWOMAN SHALL NOT BE AN HEIR WITH THE SON OF THE FREE WOMAN." So then, brethren, we are not children of a bondwoman, but of the free woman" (Galatians 4:21-30).

Instead of feeling bound to the Law given at Mount Sinai, and so feeling under obligation to observe even part of its rituals, first century Jewish Christians were no longer even at that time to reckon their relationship to be with Mount Sinai nor their affinity to be with the geographical Jerusalem in the land of Israel. And, like them, we, too, are to acknowledge 'Jerusalem above' as our 'mother.' Perhaps this comes into sharpest focus during Sunday worship. I say that because Hebrews chapters 10 & 12 teach us that God's worshipping people come to Mount Zion above and to the heavenly city of Jerusalem and in fact into the sanctuary found there. This is realized in our spiritual New Covenant collective worship experience (John 4:23,24). We should remind ourselves of what Hebrews chapter 12 says:

> "But you have come to Mount Zion and to the city of the living God, the heavenly Jerusalem, and to

> myriads of angels, to the general assembly and church of the firstborn who are enrolled in heaven, and to God, the Judge of all, and to the spirits of the righteous made perfect, and to Jesus, the mediator of a new covenant, and to the sprinkled blood, which speaks better than the blood of Abel" (Hebrews 12:22-24).

Notice the mention of the New Covenant there, connecting with the mention of the same in Galatians 4 where we started out from. But those magnificent, soaring expressions which we've just read from Hebrews 12 inform us that in some spiritual sense we approach before God each first day of every week, as his gathered people, for worship in the heavenly Jerusalem. Don't confuse the teaching here with our going to be with the Lord in heaven at his return for us. The Hebrews' letter is setting out the current operation of God's New Testament people by detailed analogy with how his Old Covenant people, Israel, once approached God in their corporate worship times. And we need to read the context starting at Hebrews chapter 8 for the true setting of this. Surely, these verses, and the revelation they contain, evoke for us the wording of Psalm 86:9: "All nations whom You have made shall come and worship before You, O Lord."

Okay, so these sections of the Bible – Galatians 4, Hebrews 12 etc. - do all seem to be connected and to offer us an explanation for the basis of Christian worship in the Church Age, this present Day of Grace. But, returning for a moment to the terms of Galatians chapter 4, how is 'Jerusalem above' the mother of believers in this age? Well, when we're born of the Spirit of God at the moment of putting our faith in Jesus Christ - after having turned away from our sins - then we're born, quite literally the Bible says, 'from above.'

We're born 'from above' - and it's certainly God's intention that we should be true 'sons of the New Covenant'. For Paul says Abraham's wife Sarah symbolizes the New Covenant in Jesus' blood. This New Covenant is identified with the Jerusalem above. Believers who are born from above have Jerusalem above for their mother and come within the scope of the New Covenant which replaced the Old Covenant God made with Israel. The Old Covenant directed Israelite paths to Zion on this earth; but now it's the highways to Zion above that should occupy our minds in this era, and command our obedience - and all this under the terms of the New Covenant made effective through Jesus' death. If only we could get a grip of the greater glory of this, there'd be no temptation for God's New Testament people to return to the mere symbols and ceremonies of the Old Testament way of worship. It's right for us to regard ourselves as 'sons of the New Covenant' - or sons of the 'freewoman' - and that makes us sons of Zion above. We mentioned Psalm 86 a moment ago, and really that psalm sets the scene for the one that follows. Psalm 87 announces:

> "His foundation is in the holy mountains. The LORD loves the gates of Zion more than all the dwellings of Jacob. Glorious things are spoken of you, O city of God! "I will make mention of Rahab and Babylon to those who know Me; behold, O Philistia and Tyre, with Ethiopia: 'This one was born there.' And of Zion it will be said, "This one and that one were born in

> her; and the Most High Himself shall establish her." The LORD will record, when He registers the peoples: "This one was born there."'

It appears that famous enemies of God's people, past and future, will in a day to come – and in terms of their believing remnants – pay tribute, as these nations' representatives flow up to Zion. They'll hail Jerusalem (see Isaiah 2) as their 'mother city.' This will happen after Christ's promised return to rule on this earth for a thousand years. The prophetic message of this psalm carries us forward to a time when the city of God's choice will finally become the centre of world-wide dominion. The absolute thrill that God has chosen Zion as his holy hill in preference to all others runs right through Psalm 87. God has set himself there simply because he loves the place. And that's the source of its glory, stability and blessing. Peace will come to Jerusalem, make no mistake.

This psalm tells of a time when some of Israel's enemies will be reborn as citizens of Zion. Egypt and Babylon, two of Israel's greatest persecutors in history, will eventually be reconciled with her - together with Philistia, an ancient enemy, along with the trading centre of Tyre, and even distant Ethiopia. This psalm with its repeated reference to Israel's major Old Testament enemies, points to earthly Zion in the first instance, reaching a fuller meaning in terms of something still future on this earth - seen also from other Bible verses - a time when Israel's peace and prosperity will again spread to surrounding lands as in the golden age of Solomon (see 1 Kings 9 & 10), only more so.

While recognizing that, in the future, nations previously hostile to Israel really will be reconciled to her, and Israel and Zion, that is, Jerusalem, will be at the head of the nations and central to the earth – yet, now, more clearly glimpsed from the New Covenant perspective in Galatians 4, we can see that when the psalmist long ago used the term 'Zion' more than one application is possible. Galatians chapter 4 in closing makes it absolutely clear that heavenly Jerusalem or spiritual Zion refers to an ultimate reality way beyond its earthly counterpart. The 'Jerusalem above' mentioned by Paul is the heavenly Zion, the original blueprint for what became established on earth. And our spiritual identity - our new Christian identity - is given to us as being from there, that is, from the original heavenly Zion. As the Apostle Paul could say to faithful disciples of Christ at Philippi: "For our citizenship is in heaven, from which we also eagerly wait for the Savior, the Lord Jesus Christ" (Philippians 3:20).

The New Testament urges us "to set our minds above" (Colossians 3:1) and it's in this sense we're encouraging each other to have our thoughts stirred towards the Zion above where the Lord Jesus Christ is already installed (Psalm 2). If the highway from Sinai to Zion demanded the obedience of Israelites long ago; how much more the highway to 'the Jerusalem which is above' ought to claim the obedience of disciples of the Lord Jesus! Only careful obedience to our Saviour's commands will bring about the kind of Christian unity the Lord had in view in giving these commands. Sadly, we vary in our obedience to the terms of the new covenant and so professing Christianity is in a divided state on the earth today

- just as the geographical city of Jerusalem is divided. How different from the heavenly reality it's designed to model!

Later still, Revelation chapter 21 tells us that God's 'tabernacle' (see Hebrews 8:1,2) will be with redeemed humanity on the new earth in the new Jerusalem - 'our present and eternal home,' as a Christian worship song says (Psalms, Hymns and Spiritual Songs, 61). The Apostle John, in Revelation chapter 21, saw the New Jerusalem coming down out of heaven from God. How wonderful to consider that our eternal theme will be our saying worshipfully to God: 'all our fountains are in You!' – 'all our springs of joy – all our sources of true joy – are found in You!' By then we'll be intensely aware that we have no other happiness than that which is found in the blessed God.

CHAPTER SEVEN: REVIEW QUESTIONS

1. How are the final verses of Galatians chapter 4 the most wonderful answer to those who wanted to turn the clock back? Is Galatians 4:30 the final answer?
2. In what sense could we say that the story behind the biblical use of the word 'Zion' is a tale of two cities? What are they?
3. Jacob (Genesis 28) was given a 'trailer,' as it were, of how the worship of God from God's earthly house was all about a special connection between earth and heaven. How does Paul and the writer to the Hebrews (assuming he was different) flesh out what the Lord announced in John 4:23,24)?
4. We've thought of Israel's future experience during the Millennium, as depicted in Psalm 87. But lying beyond that, and so beyond also our present Christian experience of worship in 'Jerusalem above,' there lies the glorious vista described in the last couple of Bible chapters. Is this depicting 'Jerusalem above' having come down to the new earth to be the sole, eternal location for worship?

CHAPTER EIGHT: THE OUTWORKING OF FAITHFULNESS THROUGH LOVE

It's good to observe things which are repeated in every chapter in a Bible letter. That surely tells us a lot about the main purpose behind its writing. For example, in First Thessalonians, the mention of the return of Christ for his Church features in every chapter usually towards the end. In Galatians, it's the cross which we meet in chapter after chapter. And no wonder, for the legalism Paul was countering detracted from the primacy and sufficiency of the cross.

But what's also emerged and registered with me, more recently, in my reading of Galatians (and isn't it so refreshing when we observe new insights in God's Word) has been the faithfulness of Christ as a recurring theme of this letter. That, too, was surely a most necessary antidote to the formalistic tendencies of the Galatian Christians. The faithfulness of Christ is nowhere more impressively shown than through the cross, the ultimate expression of his faithful love for us. Indeed, Christ's own faithful working to God's plan is the contrast made in this letter with the hopeless error of those who were relying on their own works to make themselves acceptable to God. And once they were secure in the truth of justification through faith, what Paul commends to the Galatian Christians in Galatians 5:6 is the outworking of that saving faith through loving service. Where had that been modelled for them? – in Christ's own saving career, of course.

As hard as it may be for those in any generation to accept that salvation is not based on personal works, it was as hard, if not harder, for the early Christians who'd come from a Jewish background. For a couple of thousand years beforehand, each new generation of males had been circumcised. This had previously been God's instruction for an age which was then past. The coming of Christ had brought a major change-point, and the apostle had to lay it on the line:

> "Look: I, Paul, say to you that if you accept circumcision, Christ will be of no advantage to you. I testify again to every man who accepts circumcision that he is obligated to keep the whole law. You are severed from Christ, you who would be justified by the law; you have fallen away from grace" (Galatians 5:2-4).

This was Paul's answer to those who had been saved through faith, prior to them beginning to wonder if they should then bolster it with circumcision. This passage is decisive as to the fact that there can be no mixture of any kind between grace and works. Works don't feature in how we obtain salvation; nor are they necessary for holding on to salvation afterwards.

But sometimes these verses, with which Galatians chapter 5 opens, have been distorted from their meaning and made to suggest the exact opposite of Paul's argument: that we can be severed from Christ and fall away from grace in the loss of our actual salvation! That's not at all what Paul's saying here. Instead, he says, pure reliance on Christ on the one hand, and the desire to depend in some way on human effort on the other, belong to two totally different categories - such that seeking to even maintain our salvation by some effort of our own transfers us from the one 'camp' to the other. In that sense, we're cut off from being able to proclaim 'Christ alone.' We've fallen away from the advocacy of 'grace alone.' By no longer operating in the sphere of 'Christ alone' and 'grace alone', we lose all certainty and enjoyment of the salvation that God's provided for us in the one finished work of his own son upon the cross (John 19:30).

Of course, this is what Paul consistently taught everywhere and throughout the 13 Bible letters which bear his name. You remember how he answered the Philippian jailor 'believe on the Lord Jesus Christ and you will be saved'? But just suppose for a moment that the gift of salvation is subsequently conditional upon our own good works - then we cannot possibly know if we have done well enough to still keep hold of it or not; and in that case Paul's note of confident assurance to the jailor ('you will be saved') would then ring false.

Similarly, Paul is at pains to make himself clear on this point throughout this letter to the Galatians. His detailed reasoning is against Law-keeping as a means of salvation, and equally against any religious works which try to show the standard of the Law (see Romans 2:14,15) - and the argument is equally applicable whether such works are for obtaining or maintaining salvation. Let's just skim over a few of the many points he makes. He says that any salvation which is conditional upon works would demean Christ. This point is made around verse 17 of chapter 2 where Paul argues:

> "... we know that a person is not justified by works of the law but through faith in Jesus Christ, so we also have believed in Christ Jesus, in order to be justified by faith in Christ and not by works of the law, because by works of the law no one will be justified. But if, in our endeavor to be justified in Christ, we too were found to be sinners, is Christ then a servant of sin? Certainly not!" (Galatians 2:16-17).

A works-based salvation – one where we feel we need to endeavour to add to Christ's insufficient work either to become or to remain saved – such a view of salvation demeans Christ by making him a servant of sin. Relying to some extent on our own efforts is also a view that nullifies grace, as Paul shows a few verses later in v.21, saying:

> "It is no longer I who live, but Christ who lives in me. And the life I now live in the flesh I live by faith in the Son of God, who loved me and gave himself for me. I do not nullify the grace of God, for if righteousness were through the law, then Christ died for no purpose" (Galatians 2:20-21).

If the doing of good works could in some way contribute to our salvation or to our keeping hold of it, then this makes God's grace of no account. As if these consequences weren't bad enough, Paul goes on to show that a dependence on good works in relation to being saved involves a misunderstanding of the role of God's Holy Spirit (Galatians 3:3) when he says:

> "O foolish Galatians! Who has bewitched you? It was before your eyes that Jesus Christ was publicly portrayed as crucified. Let me ask you only this: Did you receive the Spirit by works of the law or by hearing with faith? Are you so foolish? Having begun by the Spirit, are you now being perfected by the flesh?" (Galatians 3:1-3).

As he says at the beginning of Ephesians: after listening to the message of truth, the gospel of our salvation, and after having believed, we were sealed in Christ with the Holy Spirit. In other words, the Spirit's work endorsed our faith, not our works. And still Paul has even more reasons to multiply against a works-based salvation. For example, in Ephesians 3:10 he says: "For all who rely on works of the law are under a curse." Works are bound to a curse, not the blessing of salvation. What's more the Law, and its works, acted like a prison warder, like the discipline imposed by a personal tutor:

> "Now before faith came, we were held captive under the law, imprisoned until the coming faith would be revealed. So then, the law was our guardian until Christ came, in order that we might be justified by faith. But now that faith has come, we are no longer under a guardian, for in Christ Jesus you are all sons of God, through faith" (Galatians 3:23-26).

If we value what it means to be a son of God, through faith, then we'll not attribute our salvation as having anything to do with works. Finally, Paul reminds us we are not under law. Remember good works which we do are an outward showing of the law written on our hearts. But Israel's experience should've proved to us that this is no defence against our own sinful nature with all its cravings. A sanctified life is impossible without the Holy Spirit. Paul says: "Walk by the Spirit, and you will not gratify the desires of the flesh ..." (Galatians 5:16) and: "If you are led by the Spirit, you are not under the law" (Galatians 5:18).

A faith plus works formula is like trying to turn back from the Spirit to the Law as our sanctifier. Impossible! Someone confronted Martin Luther, upon the Reformer's rediscovery of the biblical doctrine of justification by faith alone – and confronted him with the remark, "If this is true, a person could simply live as he pleased!" "Indeed!" answered Luther. "Now, what pleases you?" Augustine's response on this point was similar to Luther's. What he said was: "Love God and do as you please." But don't misunderstand - this touches on the motivation the Christian has for his or her actions. The person who's been justified by God's grace has a new, higher, and nobler motivation for holiness than the shallow, hypocritical self-righteousness or fear that seems to motivate many rule-bound, works-based religious people.

CHAPTER EIGHT: REVIEW QUESTIONS

1. Why is the story of the cross, and Christ's faithful working to God's plan as shown there supremely, the recurring motif of this letter?
2. What other reasons does Paul marshal together throughout this letter all aimed at showing that either obtaining or maintaining salvation cannot be down to our own efforts? Which speaks most forcibly to you?
3. Why is the Holy Spirit more prominently described as 'Holy'? (He shares the same quality of holiness as does the Father and the Son, who are not always so described.)
4. Why is this relevant for those who advocating the Law as their sanctifier?

CHAPTER NINE: ENDING ON A PRACTICAL NOTE: THE TRUE PLACE FOR GOOD WORKS (GALATIANS 5-6)

Have you noticed the parallels that exist between the Bible letters written to the Romans and the Galatians? It shouldn't really surprise us because in each of these letters Paul is battling against the same error. In fact, the similar treatment would seem to confirm that these are the best counter-points to use against the false view that salvation is by works – perhaps even the complete set of reasons explaining why this is a misunderstanding of God's amazing grace. Let's check out the themes which the two letters (Romans & Galatians) have in common. There's ...

- the inability of the law to justify (Galatians 2:16; Romans 3:20);
- the believer's deadness to the law (Galatians 2:19; Romans 7:4);
- the believer's co-crucifixion with Christ (Galatians 2:20; Romans 6:6);
- the example given of Abraham's justification by faith (Galatians 3:6; Romans 4:3);
- the mention that believers are Abraham's spiritual children (Galatians 3:7; Romans 4:10);
- the blessing that comes as a result of this (Galatians 3:9; Romans 4:23,24);
- the clear warning that, on the contrary, the law brings

God's wrath (Galatians 3:10; Romans 4:15).

We also find mention of ...

- the universality of sin (Galatians 3:22; Romans 11:32);
- the fact that believers are baptized into Christ (Galatians 3:27; Romans 6:3);
- the clarification concerning believers' spiritual adoption (Galatians 4:5-7; Romans 814-17);
- the fact that love fulfils the law (Galatians 5:14; Romans 13:8-10);
- the emphasized importance of walking in the Spirit (Galatians 5:16; Romans 8:4);
- the warfare of the flesh against the Spirit (Galatians 5:17; Romans 7:23,25); and, finally
- the importance of bearing one another's burdens (Galatians 6:2; Romans 15:1).

That's a very abbreviated overview, but I want to turn finally now to chapters 5 and 6 of Galatians. It's there that Paul turns to more practical matters, as is often his way towards the end of his letters. His major theme has been to showcase the faithfulness of Christ over against the hopelessness of our own works as the basis of our acceptance with God. Now, he turns to explore how we too can be faithful as disciples of our faithful master. Paul stresses that the true Christian life should be characterised as "faith working through love" (Galatians 5:6); and then adds, "through love [we should be] serving one another" (v.13). Taken together, these give an attractive portrait of the essence of Christianity.

On that point emphasizing 'love,' we scan down the chapter to remind ourselves how love heads up the listing of the fruit of the Spirit in Galatians 5:

> "But I say, walk by the Spirit, and you will not carry out the desire of the flesh. For the flesh sets its desire against the Spirit, and the Spirit against the flesh; for these are in opposition to one another, so that you may not do the things that you please. But if you are led by the Spirit, you are not under the Law. Now the deeds of the flesh are evident, which are: immorality, impurity, sensuality, idolatry, sorcery, enmities, strife, jealousy, outbursts of anger, disputes, dissensions, factions, envying, drunkenness, carousing, and things like these, of which I forewarn you, just as I have forewarned you, that those who practice such things will not inherit the kingdom of God.
>
> But the fruit of the Spirit is love, joy, peace, patience, kindness, goodness, faithfulness, gentleness, self-control; against such things there is no law. Now those who belong to Christ Jesus have crucified the flesh with its passions and desires. If we live by the Spirit, let us also walk by the Spirit. Let us not become boastful, challenging one another, envying one another" (Galatians 5:16-26).

We are complete in Christ, but how do we become in daily life what we already are by the grace of God in his sight? The Bible instructs us to focus on our Christian identity and character

(Romans 8; Colossians 3; Galatians 5; 2 Peter 1). We can't do this ourselves, it's only by working with God.

Remember we said that works follow salvation, but don't produce it, and this is a work of grace in which we must be diligent. Grace is not opposed to effort, but it's only opposed to earning. So, we're to put to death, by the Spirit, the deeds of our body (Romans 8:13). Or in the language of some translations of Colossians 3, we're to mortify our earthly members – things like immorality, impurity and greed. To return again to chapter 5 of Galatians, it's the crucifying of our fallen nature with its passions and desires (v.24). In the Lord's words, it's by taking up our cross daily (Luke 9:23). We obviously need God's help, for no-one can crucify him - or herself.

Mortification is a forgotten Christian discipline, it seems, having been ignored probably due to being confused with masochism or asceticism. But it's neither about beating ourselves up or hiding ourselves away. It's about recognising evil and refusing it by setting the mind such that we can bring our body to submission such that it becomes poised to do good - not by force of will – but by spiritual disciplines which are about breaking bad habits and making good habits. It helps us to turn from evil when we make no provision for the lusts of the flesh (Romans 13:14). Negatively, it's by figuratively gouging out our eye, and cutting off our hand or foot (Matthew 5:29,30); more positively, it's by setting our mind on things above, things of the Spirit of God (Romans 8:5; Colossians 3:1; Philippians 4:8) – so it's both by putting off what's inconsistent and putting on what's consistent with the life of our risen Lord.

Daily, God's Word in the power of his Spirit enters the mind and filters down into our heart and there shapes our will to produce change in our soul. Spiritual transformation is this overall process by which all the elements of self take on the character of the elements of Christ – so that we have his mind (1 Corinthians 2:16), his emotions (even the affections of Christ Jesus, Philippians 1:8) – and so on, until the love of Christ controls us (2 Corinthians 5:14).

Having mentioned the Spirit there, I'd like to comment now on the verse which says: 'For the one who sows to his own flesh will from the flesh reap corruption, but the one who sows to the Spirit will from the Spirit reap eternal life' (Galatians 6:8). What does it mean to "sow to the Spirit"? I suggest the most helpful approach is to scan the paragraph we find this expression in, searching for clues as to what it might mean. In the surrounding texts, we find Paul dealing with such matters as gently restoring a sinning brother; assisting someone who's burdened; sharing material things with the teacher who's communicated spiritual things to us; simply doing good to all; and glorying only in the cross. It's not intended surely as an exhaustive list, but do these things not inform us of the type of activity that's consistent with "sowing to the Spirit"?

On the other hand, what might "sowing to our own flesh" look like in terms of behaviours? Using the same method, we find mention close by of having an inflated sense of importance; keeping up worldly appearances; trying to avoid being stigmatized or persecuted at all costs; and being self-congratulatory. But what does it mean that we reap eternal life from the Spirit? Don't we already have the assurance of eternal life? Yes, we do, based on, for example, 1 John 5:13 where we're told that those who believe in the name of the son of God know that they have eternal life. Does this additional reaping of eternal life then suggest to us that there's a sense in which we can enhance our eternal life?

Before we look at that, let's touch base with basics. What is eternal life? Before we received the gift of eternal life through our Lord Jesus Christ (Romans 6:23), we were dead in our sins before God (Ephesians 6:1). At that time in our experience, God meant nothing to us, we simply weren't interested in anything spiritual (or else our interest was misguided). We first detected the change God had brought about in us when we suddenly discovered an interest in God, as someone might discover an interest in art where before they were 'dead' to it. Think of how the prodigal son, in Jesus' famous story, was 'dead' to his father at the beginning, having previously no interest in relating to and communicating with him. But the time came when, upon his return, now suitably chastened, he knew what it was to enjoy a love for his father. He now felt interested in communicating with his father, and enjoying a relationship with him for the very first time in his life. The father said of the son that he'd been as one who'd been dead to him before, but it was as if he was now alive – there was now an interest, a connection, a bond.

Eternal life is cultivating a friendship in which God remains loyal to us for ever, unaffected by our death (2 Corinthians 5:1). Now, it's quite a thrust of the New Testament (in, for example, the pastoral letters to Timothy and Titus) that we can make adjustments in view of the coming day of Christ. Does this mean that we can 'upgrade' our eternal life experience? Well, for sure, we can get to know God better, starting now – after all that was the Apostle Paul's passionate desire (Philippians 3:10). And, what's more, he tells us that godliness is profitable for all things, since it holds promise for the present life and also for the life to come (1 Timothy 4:7,8).

It does seem, then, that although our eternal life is assured to us as a free gift – not the result of our own performance-based obedience - we can, however, get a stronger grip on eternal life. I hope our study of Galatians has helped us in that.

CHAPTER NINE: REVIEW QUESTIONS

1. Do you detect any similarities between the books of Romans and Galatians? Are there any differences of emphasis that strikes you?
2. How would you sum up the essence of Christianity?
3. Crucifying the flesh, or mortification, is something raised here in common with Romans and Colossians (and the Lord's words in the Gospels). Do you have any program for it in your life? Do you agree it should be a discipline which we practice?
4. Can you elaborate upon how we 'reap eternal life' (Galatians 6:8)?
5. Grace is opposed to earning, but not to effort. How is that an important practical distinction?

Did you love *Amazing Grace! Paul's Gospel Message to the Galatians*? Then you should read *Christ-centred Faith*[1] by Brian Johnston!

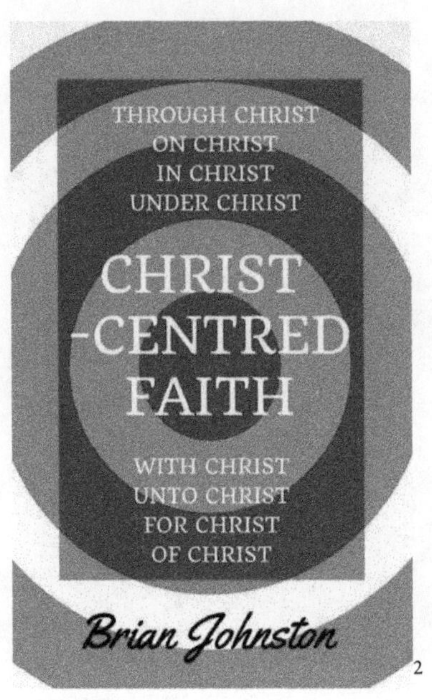

THROUGH CHRIST
ON CHRIST
IN CHRIST
UNDER CHRIST
CHRIST
-CENTRED
FAITH
WITH CHRIST
UNTO CHRIST
FOR CHRIST
OF CHRIST
Brian Johnston

[2]

As Brian Johnston explains, 8 different prepositions are used in the Holy Spirit's inspiration of the apostle Paul's writings, and this is no accident for each of them tells us something different about our relationship with Jesus.

Also included is a bonus book "Faith with Focus" which looks at four "one things" that the Bible talks about.

CHAPTER ONE: THROUGH CHRIST (OUR MEDIATOR)

---

1. https://books2read.com/u/bxgL6v

2. https://books2read.com/u/bxgL6v

Also by Brian Johnston

Healthy Churches - God's Bible Blueprint For Growth
Hope for Humanity: God's Fix for a Broken World
First Corinthians: Nothing But Christ Crucified
Bible Answers to Listeners' Questions
Living in God's House: His Design in Action
Christianity 101: Seven Bible Basics
Nights of Old: Bible Stories of God at Work
Daniel Decoded: Deciphering Bible Prophecy
A Test of Commitment: 15 Challenges to Stimulate Your Devotion to Christ
John's Epistles - Certainty in the Face of Change
If Atheism Is True...
8 Amazing Privileges of God's People: A Bible Study of Romans 9:4-5
Learning from Bible Grandparents
Increasing Your Christian Footprint
Christ-centred Faith
Mindfulness That Jesus Endorses
Amazing Grace! Paul's Gospel Message to the Galatians
Abraham: Friend of God
The Future in Bible Prophecy
Unlocking Hebrews
Learning How To Pray - From the Lord's Prayer

About the Bush: The Five Excuses of Moses
The Five Loves of God
Deepening Our Relationship With Christ
Really Good News For Today!
A Legacy of Kings - Israel's Chequered History
Minor Prophets: Major Issues!
The Tabernacle - God's House of Shadows
Tribes and Tribulations - Israel's Predicted Personalities
Once Saved, Always Saved - The Reality of Eternal Security
After God's Own Heart : The Life of David
Jesus: What Does the Bible Really Say?
God: His Glory, His Building, His Son
The Feasts of Jehovah in One Hour
Knowing God - Reflections on Psalm 23
Praying with Paul
Get Real ... Living Every Day as an Authentic Follower of Christ
A Crisis of Identity
Double Vision: Hidden Meanings in the Prophecy of Isaiah
Samson: A Type of Christ
Great Spiritual Movements
Take Your Mark's Gospel
Total Conviction - 4 Things God Wants You To Be Fully Convinced About
Esther: A Date With Destiny
Experiencing God in Ephesians
James - Epistle of Straw?
The Supremacy of Christ
The Visions of Zechariah
Encounters at the Cross
Five Sacred Solos - The Truths That the Reformation Recovered

Kingdom of God: Past, Present or Future?

Overcoming Objections to Christian Faith

Stronger Than the Storm - The Last Words of Jesus

Fencepost Turtles - People Placed by God

Five Woman and a Baby - The Genealogy of Jesus

Pure Milk - Nurturing New Life in Jesus

Jesus: Son Over God's House

Salt and the Sacrifice of Christ

The Glory of God

The Way: Being a New Testament Disciple

Power Outage - Christianity Unplugged

Windows to Faith: Insights for the Inquisitive

Home Truths

60 Minutes to Raise the Dead

About the Author

Born and educated in Scotland, Brian worked as a government scientist until God called him into full-time Christian ministry on behalf of the Churches of God (www.churchesofgod.info). His voice has been heard on Search For Truth radio broadcasts for over 30 years (visit www.searchfortruth.podbean.com) during which time he has been an itinerant Bible teacher throughout the UK and Canada. His evangelical and missionary work outside the UK is primarily in Belgium and The Philippines. He is married to Rosemary, with a son and daughter.

About the Publisher

Hayes Press (www.hayespress.org) is a registered charity in the United Kingdom, whose primary mission is to disseminate the Word of God, mainly through literature. It is one of the largest distributors of gospel tracts and leaflets in the United Kingdom, with over 100 titles and hundreds of thousands despatched annually. In addition to paperbacks and eBooks, Hayes Press also publishes Plus Eagles Wings, a fun and educational Bible magazine for children, and Golden Bells, a popular daily Bible reading calendar in wall or desk formats. Also available are over 100 Bibles in many different versions, shapes and sizes, Bible text posters and much more!

www.ingramcontent.com/pod-product-compliance
Lightning Source LLC
Chambersburg PA
CBHW021211020426
42331CB00003B/303

* 9 7 8 1 3 9 3 7 2 6 7 5 3 *